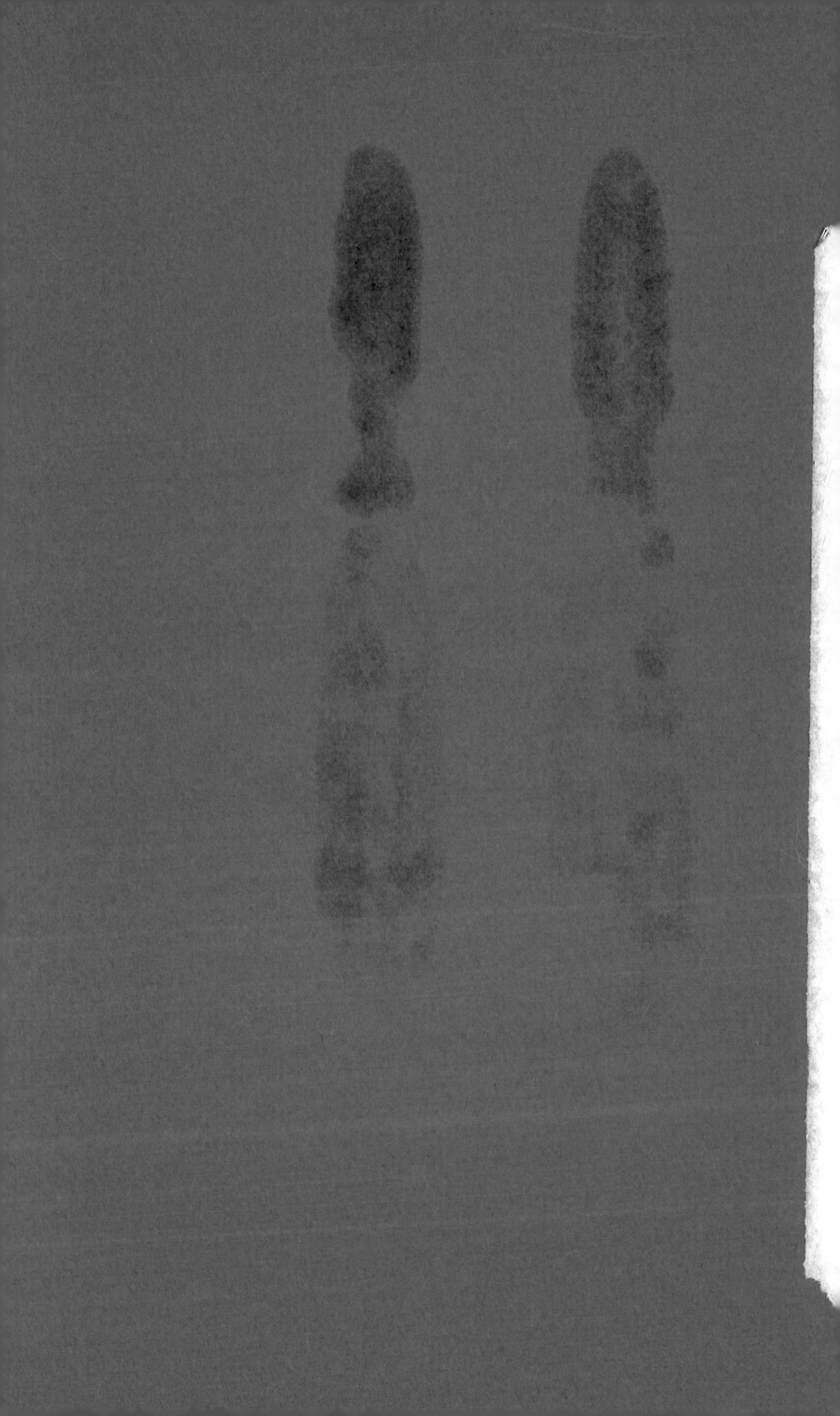

ALMA TO HER SISTER

alone no loneliness in the dream in the quiet
in the sunrise in the sunset Louise.
in the dream no loneliness in the dream
in the sunrise in the sunset just the two of us

alone no loneliness done. in the dream
in the quiet of the day done in the sunrise
Louise. in the dream in the dream
in the sunrise in the sunset.

alone no loneliness done. no loneliness
in the dream in the quiet
in the sunrise in the sunset. Louise
in the dream. in the sunrise in the sunset.

SKYLORD

for Harold Gregg (1906–1980)

The small hawk flutters fiercely upright,
shivering with great energy to stand so
in air over hills and their declivities.
Hunting mole, mouse and whom. Ally of wind,
owner of sky, elegant lord embracing what is
known and not known. A magnificence over us
which plunges for small life to eat. Dear gods,
you are dependent on the mouse that lives
with the hill's heartbeat and knows more,
much more by far, than your invisible school
of latitude and longitude. You must study
by compression of patience movement between
eyelids blinking. Must learn racing between
two heartbeats. And it takes you a long while
and humility and failure. Each time you come
close we look in awe of you that the sky too
has its stomachs to feed and must come down
to us and learn our ways. For you do. With
splendor and work you learn how to kill and take
what you must while the salmon rot after spawning
in rain and in clarity. As we learn hovering
and density from your necessity. We learn
from you joy in the ground as you raise each
prey in your claws from the dear lost earth.

SUN MOON KELP FLOWER OR GOAT

Later I would say, I have cut myself free from order,
statistics, and what not, what have you.
But I was never connected. To anything.
Marriage taught me to let go more. As if I knew
what I wanted. As if I were after something.
The *finally* was that year as I walked the island
every day. I could feel something extraordinary.
It was the same in me as outside me. I could say us:
The flat land I walked. The mountain approaching.
The blanching of everything living and dying.
Ruined hills and towns without roofs on the houses.
Men and women in black clothing offering water,
singing, being silent, laughing. Dying, as if that
were anything to us who were nature and beyond
suffering. What survives. The part which remains.
What is birth and death to sun, fish, kelp, eggs?
But there is kindness which feeds us another way,
with windlessness, empty heat, or the taste of grapes.

AS WHEN THE
BLOWFISH PERISHING

As when the blowfish, perishing,
makes itself the greatest size,
the empty agoras and broken colosseums
repeat the supposition of a god
who worshipped a god. Pretending
those men were proportionate
to what they made. And they are. I think
of how you dream and dream and care
for the blood carried in silver bowls
out of the room. Of my diminishing
as the world makes love to me.
It is a long way from the rock to here.
There is a huge pile of dead people
and they will not sing. I wish so
you would come back.
We kept the courtesy an internal form
to have the beauty after.

III

A woman comes to my door and asks for bread.
It is winter. I look at her face
and recognize myself. I say: Lady, you hurt me
with your pain. She sings: Are you afraid
when the branches scrape the window panes?
Are you? Never has there been more agreement
between anyone. Go away, I say. Go away.
And slam the door. I fall down crying
for anything but woman to ease my suffering.
Death would be more kind. I open the door.
She is standing there with tears on her face,
just like before. Unsure whether to start again.

IV

Statuary used to fill the gardens of rich
and powerful men. At the end in Paris
they were of women. That is all gone now.
The wars came. Lists of dead were horrible.
I walk through the fields of rotting bodies
at evening to get a bucket of water
to carry back to the house on my head.
Gradually there will be gardens again.
First for food and then also for flowers.

LILITH

I

The light is on my body also.
Even now when I am alone in the woods.
That is something they never tell you.
And I have always been alone.
Even when men found me and used me,
it never lasted. I knew lust
can be satisfied and I would be
returned to myself before long.
Would see everything as it was.
Dark trees, bright lights.
Speech only was lost.

II

I line up five stones on the ground.
I count them. I laugh
even though I am alone.
Remembering how the men never knew
how reasonable I am. Every day
I walk to the edge of the world
and look at the ocean.
And then return to my home.
It goes on like this.
They are afraid of the pain
they have given me. I made a dam
in the creek today and then took
the stones away. I make a fire
to keep warm when it is necessary.
How can they think I am crazy?

STAYING ON

The geese go over
with a broken sound,
moving clumsily toward
their Troy. As she,
crouched down,
goes on picking
up the apples
under the trees.
Not proceeding anywhere.
Close to the ground
with bobcats, rabbits,
mice, woodchucks,
a doe with her young.
Arriving their way
into winter.

Are you lost if there is no recognition?
Is beauty home? Is fear or pain?
An old man who drives the truck and has a farm
of his own down the road said,
'I just help during the harvest.
I have everything except apples. Lots of squash.'
It made me happy to know they still say harvest.

I am here with them for the harvest. Thirty-six.
A woman. Canning when there's time. It will be
very cold soon. Already there are dark rains.

the apple trees all day. I saw two night hawks
white with black wave designs counter to the wings.
The boss saw two hundred of them fly over
this valley once. Going south.
What if I continue unnoticed.

Foxes red and grey. Woodchucks. A pretty rabbit
on the road in the rain, confused and afraid.
Running suddenly toward the lights.

An apple has all colors. Even blue.
Much purple and maroon. (If there would be
no recognition and the world remains far away?)
The leaves are a duller green than the grass.
I pick macintosh, but there are forty kinds
on the land around. Three hundred acres
near the next town. This is autumn in Massachusetts.
Not my home. I heard of beauty in New England
and the people. Came looking for love.

Nobody talks to the Jamaicans. They are driven
to Safeway in the bus and brought back.
I saw one alone just standing by the woods.
'I send money to my mother if I feel like it,'
he said to impress me. About eighteen.
He will cut cane for the first time this year.
'I hear the bosses are mean,' I said.
'We make more money,' he said. 'It is a longer time.'

WHAT IF THE WORLD STAYS
ALWAYS FAR OFF

What if the world is taken from me?
If there is no recognition? My words unheard?
Keats wanted to write great poetry
and I am in the orchard all day.

The work is too hard and no one here
will do it. So they bring Jamaicans.
The men sometimes sing on their ladders.
Named Henry and George. 'Yes, Boss,' they say.
The bus brought them late this morning.
They not wanting to work because of the cold.
They walk slowly through the wet grass.
'Today we are not happy,' they say going by me.

The grass is wet one to three hours.
Then dry. Sometimes everything is warm
and I wish the man I know would come
in his car and make love to me.

We do not speak much. Because of the work.
And because I am the only woman.
They see no women. Two months here picking apples.
Six in Florida cutting cane.

At night my body is so tired I don't want
to make love. I want to be alone and to sleep.
It is very beautiful in the fields under

THIS PLACE

There is a place in the desert which I keep making,
making the light blister and the shadows glow
with a red darkness. Making black a substance
invisible behind the red. Shadows
like those in a place built to be a stronghold
for pity's sake make me wonder why I put it there,
making sure of the heat and the blond lions
quivering against the blond sandstone so that
you almost cannot see them, or believe them
a mirage. Making water of them and moving them
closer to the rock. It makes me wonder why
I saw lions as guardians, angels flexing their jaws,
tightening against the walls for pity's sake.
And I cry out to them with my burned mouth
full of joy and wonder: 'Pity, I have found you.
Pity, I bring you a present of my mind, complete
with the sweet smell of the King's garden
when you come into it from a small distance.
I have not made you up. You are here.'
And the lions turn in the canyon I have made
with my voice, see me calling, and we move closer.

THE GRUB

The almost transparent white grub moves
slowly along the edge of the frying pan.
The grease makes the only sound, loud
in the empty room. Even the rim is cooking him.
The worm stops. Raises his head slightly.
Lowers it, moving tentatively down the side.
He seems to be moving on his own time,
but he is falling by definition. He moves forward
touching the frying grease with his whole face.

The world gives forth beauty
like the great, glad women in the dream.
It overwhelms us. Spills over.
I am afraid the earth will take it back
and part of my self will get lost
and I will not be a fitting gift.

The gods must not know us well or they would
not dance so openly, so happily before us.

THE GODS MUST NOT KNOW US

The signifying clouds at dawn
fill me. Open my spirit.
The shining of sun and moon
morning after morning
makes my heart serene.
(from SHANG-SHU TA CHUAN by Fu Sheng)

All the different kinds of light
give off light.
The light of the heart (sun).
The light of the mind (moon).
Longing and having make it all
possible for us.

But what the world gives disturbs,
this confusion of excess the world gives.
Morning comes again and again,
holding everything lovingly.
We cannot hold it all at once
this giving.

KALOS is written over the heads of the gods
on the Greek vases. They like beauty so much
they fill the world with it.
Until the plenty makes our joy hesitate
and I fear they will know we do not have a place
big enough to handle so much.

Blake comes down, calling me.
Says this is the time.
The sea is hitting the rocks.
The light is crushed and flies up,
back to the sun.
Rejoice in the breaking of the light.
Rejoice when you are two and one.
In the leaving and the coming home.
Rejoice in the room that awaits you,
empty except for the empty glass.

I fly up. Disappear inside of him.
It is grand. I see the simple cow,
a red-tailed hawk and a lamb.
The creek with the small fish in it,
and sounds of the sea at the edge of a field.
The sound of it lightly under the trees.
Birds whistling. Wind and leaves mixing
in the slightly swollen heat.
The sound of the sea in his mind.

The glass is spilling.
They both shine in that room,
water and spilling light.

BLAKE

The sun is on the roof,
the laundry is drying in the light.
Air moves around me and I prepare.
Make a gift of myself. Make my feet soft,
and think of Blake riding
near the tops of the trees
past our house.

The bread is in the oven and we die.
The day is spread and we delay.
Blake already is in the sky.
What is joy in this dark room?
What is light to this?
All night the ghosts of disperse,
of chaos, flee through my dreaming.

I would not repent. Though the world
separated into all its parts
and could not go back.
Get out! Get out! Get out! I shouted,
until I could not tell if anything was left
to talk to that had ears. Still refused.
Then the sun smiled, and Christ smiled,
and my laundry grew soft in the warm wind.
There. See there. The world is good to me.
I am finished with knife and window.
My bed will be underground soon enough.
I will persist in this permanence
that flesh holds. The body smooth,
the voices speaking within.

NOT SINGING

When you stop looking at the garden,
the eye begins furtively to acknowledge the barren poplars
and the giant spruce and the firs.
And so it is with this maid in me not asking to be saved.
Another one takes her place. Neither merciful nor unmerciful.
There are almost no flowers to be looked at anyhow.
No flowers to bear having an opinion about.
And the more it rains the less flowers there are.
The flowers, they say, all along were the journey.
Like the branches thrown down before the little donkey feet
of Christ on the way to glory.
I would not have it different.
Ruin is everywhere. The plague of soft rain endless.
We sing of loss because the only voice they gave us
was song and reasoning. It is not love we are after.
No love. Not singing. But a somber thing.
A going to the opening and entering.

PART

III

AFTER THAT.

THE APPARENT

When I say transparency, I don't mean seeing through.
I mean the way a symbol is made when X is drawn over O.
As the world moves when it is named. In the sense
of truth by consciousness, which we translate as *opposites*.
The space we breathe is also called distance.
Presence gives. Absence allows and calls,
until Presence holds the invisible, weeping.
Transparent in the way the heart sees old leaves.
As we become more like the hills by feeling.
I mean permanence. As when the deer and I
regard each other. Ah, there was no fear then.
When she went with her young from the meadow
back into the nearly night of the woods,
it was because the rain came down suddenly harder.

TOO BRIGHT TO SEE

Just before dark the light gets dark. Violet
where my hands pull weeds around the Solomon seals.
I see with difficulty what before was easy.
Perceive what I saw before
but with more tight effort. I am moon
to what I am doing and what I was.
It is a real beauty that I lived
and dreamed would be, now know
but never then. Can tell by looking hard,
feeling which is weed and what is form.
My hands are intermediary. Neither lover
nor liar. Sweet being, if you are anywhere that hears,
come quickly. I weep, face set, no tears, mouth open.

What does the moth think when the skin begins to split?
Is the air an astonishing pain? I keep seeing the arms
bent. The legs smashed up against the breasts,
with her sex showing. The weak hands clenched.
I see the sad, unused face. Then she starts to stand up
in the opening out. I know ground and trees.
I know air. But then everything else stops
because I don't know what happens after that.

THE DEFEATED

I sat at the desk for a while fooling with my hair
and looking at the black birds on the bakery roof.
Pulled the curtain, put my hair back, and said
it's time to start. Now it's after three.
You are still on the bus, I guess, looking out
the window. Sleeping. Knowing your defeat
and eating lunch part by part so it will last
the whole journey.

I heard there are women who light candles
and put them in the sand. Wade out in dresses
carrying flowers. Here we have no hope.
The pregnant woman has the abortion and then
refuses to speak. Horses stall in their strength,
whitening patches of air with their breath.
There will be this going on without them.
Dogs bark or five birds fly straight up
to a branch out of reach.

I had warm pumpernickel bread, cheese and chicken.
It is sunny outside. I miss you. My head is tired.
John was nice this morning. Already what I remember
most is the happiness of seeing you. Having tea.
Falling asleep. Waking up with you there awake
in the kitchen. It was like being alive twice.
I'll try to tell you better when I am stronger.

II

There is nothing like that here.
Just the rain, the road, the dim
morning light, and the birds singing
faster and faster.
I follow the river with my mind,
trying to learn feeling. When I lived
at Monolithos a man rode a burro
every morning and evening
to a church that was never used,
to keep the lamps lit.
He will continue doing that
even though I came back to America.

NOW DESTROYED

I

The girl you speak of is lost,
managing to hold on only to objects
with a wildness like pleading.
Small things.
Those she can carry with her
and care for. She does not want a plant.
It might die. She prefers photographs
of the Kore with dark eyes.
The Reims Christ ('now destroyed').
A painting of an island when the sun,
going away, left the earth and Aegean
feminine for an hour.
What living is to her is painful.
Knowing life a dependency on things
which can be taken away, or forgotten.
She could be found dead in her urine
and they might throw everything out.

Oh, if you knew what you do not know
I could be in the world remembering this.
I did not cry as much in the darkness
as I will when we part in the dimness
near the opening which is the way in for you
and was the way out for me, my love.

EURYDICE

I linger, knowing you are eager (having seen
the strange world where I live)
to return to your friends
wearing the bells and singing the songs
which are my mourning.
With the water in them, with their strange rhythms.
I know you will not take me back.
Will take me almost to the world,
but not out to house, color, leaves.
Not to the sacred world that is so easy
for you, my love.

Inside my mind and in my body is a darkness
which I am equal to, but my heart is not.
Yesterday you read the Troubadour poets
in the bathroom doorway
while I painted my eyes for the journey.
While I took tiredness away from my face,
you read of that singer in a garden
with the woman he swore to love forever.

You were always curious what love is like.
Wanted to meet me, not bring me home.
Now you whistle, putting together
the new words, learning the songs
to tell the others how far you traveled for me.
Singing of my desire to live.

NO MORE MARRIAGES

Well, there ain't going to be no more marriages.
And no goddam honeymoons. Not if I can help it.
Not that I don't like men,
being in bed with them and all. It's the rest.
And that's what happens, isn't it? All those people
that get littler together. I want things
to happen to me the proper size.
The moon and the salmon and me and the fir trees
they're all the same size and they live together.
I'm the worse part, but mean no harm.
I might scare a deer, but I walk and breathe
as quiet as a person can learn.
If I'm not like my grandmother's garden
that smelled sweet all over and was warm
as a river, I do go up the mountain
to see the birds close and look
at the moon just come visible and lie down
to look at it with my face open.
Guilty or not, though, there won't be no post
cards made up of my life with Delphi on them.
Not even if I have to eat alone all those years.
They're never going to do that to me.

AFTER THAT

When the sun goes down and the world starts
to darken the three white geese do not.
Until the night really comes and covers them,
they are still white. Only perhaps waxier.

UNACCOUNTABLE

—They meant her to last forever.
—She invariably did kill someone every
        voyage she made.
—She was unaccountable.
    (Conrad, THE BRUTE)

Many things are made of pride.
She will be alone in her bath washing off
some man's sweat before you come home.
You know what power the brute has now.
There is nothing to do against it.
The husband comes home
and if he is in a good mood
goes to her,
thinking of excitement.
She lifts her arms with a cunning smile
and he licks the sweat off her sides
and belly.
She pinches off a short dark hair
stuck by her navel and they laugh.
The laugh dies.
And the next joke dies
until neither can laugh fast enough,
for silence invades the empty heart
and the ripe roses are somewhere displaced
in the memory
and the instincts run backwards.
The woman stares.
In the empty room she suddenly turns,
prepared to hear.
The husband looks down at his feet
as if trying to remember.

SUMMER IN A SMALL TOWN

When the men leave me,
they leave me in a beautiful place.
It is always late summer.
When I think of them now
I think of the place.
And being happy alone afterwards.
This time it's Clinton, New York.
I swim in the public pool
at six when the other people
have gone home.
The sky is grey, the air hot.
I walk back across the mown lawn
loving the smell and the houses
so completely it leaves my heart empty.

GROWING UP

I am reading Li Po. The T.V. is on
with the sound off.
I've seen this movie before.
I turn on the sound just for a moment
when the man says, 'I love you.'
Then turn it off and go on reading.

WHOLE AND WITHOUT
BLESSING

What is beautiful alters, has undertow.
Otherwise I have no tactics to begin with.
Femininity is a sickness. I open my eyes
out of this fever and see the meaning
of my life clearly. A thing like a hill.
I proclaim myself whole and without blessing,
or need to be blessed. A fish of my own
spirit. I belong to no one. I do not move.
Am not required to move. I lie naked on a sheet
and the indifferent sun warms me.
I was bred for slaughter, like the other
animals. To suffer exactly at the center,
where there are no clues except pleasure.

ALMA WATCHING HER HUSBAND

Halfway through the scene I could not decide
whether Alma should react or go on standing there
by the window of her dark room, her back to us
and the bright summer night above the roofs beyond.
She was looking into the apartment across the courtyard
as they finished making love and the woman
climbed down the ladder from the high bed,
shining in the candlelight. Maybe Alma
should lie on the floor with her face showing.
Or smash the tulips, kneel crying alongside,
then quickly sweep them up. But I wanted something
more tenuous. I went outside. The air smelled
like cardamom. Students were singing in the street.
It was already morning. I wrote it all down:
the kind of daylight at midnight in Denmark
and the kind at four in the morning. Maybe Alma
would sit with her legs out the window watching
the birds overhead. When I got back, the man downstairs
was crying because his wife had just died of cancer.
He used to grab Alma when she came home from ballet class
and weep in her hair. Maybe I could show Alma's husband
for the ending. Walking across the city,
over the bridges and along the moats to his workroom.
He would make soup and put it on the cast iron stove.
Pour tea and begin to work. A boy might come by
from the next cabin and say they had moved the trumpet
player into a soundproof room facing out on the marsh.
Then I knew she would just go on standing there.

CLASSICISM

The nights are very clear in Greece.
When the moon is round we see it completely
and have no feeling.

TOGETHER IN GREECE

I was sitting on the steps of the cinema
when he introduced his pretty friend.
The few bare bulbs showed how dark and barren it was.
I got up and left the town.
Went out with no attitude prepared.
I went to a winnowing ring in the fields and lay down,
where all day they ran horses and donkeys
over the barley, a farmer running with his hands tied
to them. Knew the air was cold and I saw myself there.
Realized I was strange.
When the moon wanted me to sing
with my mouth open, I refused.
I knew Jack was looking for me. Stayed silent.
Heard him calling my name in the village streets.
Finally came out of the fields
and walked toward him. Dark and huge.
My head ached from the sounds I did not make.
It was more frightening than living.
I went to him, with that singing in me.

THE SMALL LIZARD

My lizard just beyond the lamp's shine
is a gentle lizard.
Is the color of an old peach.
Has lived with me all summer
and kept his tail.

(I am a little better, but love is leaving.
I who never loved birds am growing wings.)

When I move, my lizard does not.
But watches and makes himself ready.
The moon has gone above my window now,
and will go over the roof top.

(Now, when I could help, I hold back.
My heart is sad, not wanting to fly.
Who moves from grace by choice?).

We are three stages. The lizard,
more than I or the moon, is the soul
developed. The moon will dim
and I will change;
but this immortal lizard will stay
breathing in this stone room,
without evidence.

TROUBLE IN THE PORTABLE MARRIAGE

'What whiteness will you add to this whiteness, what candor?'

We walk the dirt road toward town through the clear evening.
The sky is apricot behind the black cane. Pink above,
and dull raspberry on the Turkish hills across the water.
The Aegean is light by the shore, then dark farther out.
I cannot distinguish now which is light and which is color.
I go up the road on my bicycle, floating in the air:
the moon enlarging and decreasing moving all the time
close to my head. I stop at the bridge.
Get off and sit on the rail because I remember
I have no money. After a while you come.
Your hand touches me and then withdraws.
We talk about why the moon changes size, and I think
how I'd smelled it. Like sweet leaf smoke,
like sweet wood burning. We go toward town together,
me riding and you walking. Feeling the silk and paleness
of the air. No one passes us the whole length of the road.

THE ISLAND OF KOS

Nothing but wilderness around.
Two days of spring and then days of cold.
The sea flooding the road.
Wild heaving against poetry.
Breaking boats on the rocks.
Spill, spill and pour against the mountain.
Flooding the winter wheat.

Wait for me! Wait for me! You are far ahead.
I think the wilderness has won. We are silent
in the house while the wind rises and wanes.
I came here not knowing there was something
that could be lost. That could be taken.

In order to get to sleep, I think:
Go to sleep little goat. Your first week is over.
Go to sleep now.

THE WIFE

My husband sucks her tits.
He walks into the night, her Roma, his being alive.
Toward that outer love. I wait in the hotel
until four. I lurch from the bed
talking to myself, watch my face in the mirror.
I change my eyes, making them darker.
Take it easy, I say. It is a long time to wait in,
this order of reality. My presence stings.
I grow specific without consequence.

PART II

THE MARRIAGE AND AFTER

DIFFERENT NOT LESS

All of it changes at evening
equal to the darkening,
so that night-things may have their time.
Each gives over where its nature is essential.
The river loses all but a sound.
The bull keeps only its bulk.
Some things lose everything.
Colors are lost. And trees mostly.
At a time like this we do not doubt our dreams.
We believe the dead are standing along the other edge
of the river, but do not go to meet them.
Being no more powerful than they were before.
We see this change is for the good,
that there is completion, a coming around.
And we are glad for the amnesty.
Modestly we pass our dead in the dark,
and history—the Propylaea to the right
and above our heads. The sun, bull-black
and ready to return, holds back so the moon,
delicate and sweet, may finish her progress.
We look into the night, or death, our loss,
what is not given. We see another world alive
and our wholeness finishing.

ALMA IN ALL SEASONS

She has arms instead of breasts.
And there are no stars.
I put her in this box
because it is summer.
And put a cloth with flowers
sewn on it over her. Rabbit fur
under and around her sides.
To make summer for her.
She is not warm automatically.
The stationary box is light blue.
The jar with water holding roses
is turquoise. I see her looking out.
Her eyes are dark. Hot air sucks
my curtain out the window
and lets it drop.
Her eyes look on nothing.
She must be thinking. She must be
feeling. She does not remember people.
It is summer but the same was true
when there was snow.

GOETHE'S DEATH MASK

The face is quite smooth
everywhere except the eyes,
which are bulges
like ant hills someone tried to draw
eyes on. It is normal, of course,
that the mouth is shut
like a perfect sentence.
But there is nothing of Italy
or the rooms. As though it were
all a lie. As if he had not fed there
at all. I suppose there was never a choice.
If the happiness lasts,
it is the smoothness. The part
we do not notice. The language he made
was from the bruises. What lasted
are the eyes. Something ugly
and eaten into. What a mess his eyes are.

THE POET GOES ABOUT HER BUSINESS

for Michele (1966-1972)

Michele has become another dead little girl. An easy poem.
Instant Praxitelean. Instant seventy-five year old photograph
of my grandmother when she was a young woman with shadows
I imagine were blue around her eyes. The beauty of it.
Such guarded sweetness. What a greed of bruised gardenias.
Oh Christ, whose name rips silk, I have seen raw cypresses
so dark the mind comes to them without color.
Dark on the Greek hillside. Dark, volcanic, dry and stone.
Where the oldest women of the world are standing dressed in black
up in the branches of fig trees in the gorge
knocking with as much quickness as their weakness will allow.
Weakness which my heart must not confuse with tenderness.
And on the other side of the island a woman
walks up the path with a burden of leaves on her head,
guiding the goats with sounds she makes up,
and then makes up again. The other darkness is easy:
the men in the dreams who come in together to me with knives.
There are so many traps, and many look courageous.
The body goes into such raptures of obedience.
But the huge stones on the desert resemble
nobody's mother. I remember the snake.
After its skin had been cut away, and it was dropped
it started to move across the clearing.
Making its beautiful waving motion.
It was all meat and bone. Pretty soon it was covered with dust.
It seemed to know exactly where it wanted to go.
Toward any dark trees.

SIGISMUNDO

The fete confused me. Guests played the part of gods.
There was a woman with white skin who stood
with her pale robe open all night throwing roses.
A lady found me in the only quiet room and demanded
I take her to him. I refused even when she begged,
and went down by the water to think of something else.
Sun rose that morning on the torches.
Cool air over the tepid sea. Sigismundo the Beautiful.
Out for himself. Torturer of doves. A killer of cities.
Killer of wife before breakfast. Sigismundo,
who built a church to a woman not beautiful,
with roses cut in the stone.
All through my boyhood I was told I'd walk hand in hand
with death. I chose the good, and cried
when they marred the statues.
But there is nothing, nothing to say about my life.
Unmerciful Sigismundo did many wrongs and his people loved him
and he will live forever. I who go down like Persephone
with my accomplishments of silence and weeping unrecorded,
even I if I were a girl would answer Yes, I know how to swim.
Lie for the chance to drown in that blue water of his.
Sigismundo.

Ah, world, I love you with all my heart.
Outside the open window, down near the Hudson,
I can hear a policeman talking to another
through the car radio. It's eleven stories down
so it must be pretty loud.
The sheep, the tree, the dog, and the man
are perfectly at peace. And my peace is at peace.
Time and the earth lie down wonderfully together.

The blacks probably do rape the whites in jail
as Bill said in the coffee shop watching the game
between Oakland and Cincinnati. And no doubt
Karl was right that we should have volunteered
as victims under the bombing of Hanoi.

A guy said to Mishkin, 'If you've seen all that,
how can you go on saying you're happy?'

THE BECKETT KIT

I finally found a way of using the tree.
If the man is lying down with the sheep
while the dog stands, then the wooden tree
can also stand, in the back, next to the dog.

They show their widest parts
(the dog sideways, the tree frontal)
so that being next to each other
they function as a landscape.

I tried for nearly two months to use the tree.
I tried by putting the man,
standing of course, very far from the sheep
but in more or less the same plane.
At one point I had him almost off the table
and still couldn't get the tree to work.
It was only just now I thought of a way.

I dropped the wooden sheep from a few inches
above the table so they wouldn't bounce.
Some are on their backs but they serve
the same as the ones standing.
What I can't get over is their coming right
inadvertently when I'd be content with any solution.

AT THE SHORE

Naked women are being dragged
down the sandstone shelving
on their backs, very slowly.
With ropes tied to each foot separately
so the legs close and spread open
as they are moved.
When they cry out or shout down
at the men sitting in the lifeguard chairs
looking at them through the gun sights,
the sounds, no matter how angry or foul,
curve and billow like a wave: coming
to the men on a soft wind
caressingly, like sirens singing.

THE WOMAN WHO LOOKS FOR
HER LOST SISTER SHE SAYS

She walks all the time in the Heart Ward.
She makes no sound. She is always alone.
If she is looking in the toilet stall and you come in
she leaves. She calls you Dear.
I was thinking of giving her my flowers.
Just now she came over and said,
'You don't have to be writing all the time Dear.'
I said, 'Do you have any flowers?'
She said, 'No Dear.'
I said, 'Do you want any flowers?'
She said, 'No, no flowers Dear.'
I said, 'Don't you want any flowers at all?'
'No,' she said, 'it's too late for flowers Dear.'

THERE SHE IS

When I go into the garden, there she is.
The specter holds up her arms to show
that her hands are eaten off.
She is silent because of the agony.
There is blood on her face.
I can see she has done this to herself.
So she would not feel the other pain.
And it is true, she does not feel it.
She does not even see me.
It is not she any more, but the pain itself
that moves her. I look and think
how to forget. How can I live while she
stands there? And if I take her life
what will that make of me? I cannot
touch her, make her conscious.
It would hurt her too much.
I hear the sound all through the air
that was her eating, but it is on its own now,
completely separate from her. I think
I am supposed to look. I am not supposed
to turn away. I am supposed to see each detail
and all expression gone. My God, I think,
if paradise is to be here
it will have to include her.

GNOSTICS ON TRIAL

Let us make the test. Say God wants you
to be unhappy. That there is no good.
That there are horrors in store for us
if we do manage to move toward Him.
Say you keep Art in its place, not too high.
And that everything, even eternity, is measurable.
Look at the photographs of the dead,
both natural (one by one) and unnatural
in masses. All tangled. You know about that.
And can put Beauty in its place. Not too high,
and passing. Make love our search for unhappiness,
which is His plan to help us.
Disregard that afternoon breeze from the Aegean
on a body almost asleep in the shuttered room.
Ignore melons, and talking with friends.
Try to keep from rejoicing. Try
to keep from happiness. Just try.

This song comes from the bottom of the hill at night, in summer.
From a distance as fine as that first light on those islands.
As the lights on the dark island which held still while our ship
came away. This is the love song that lasts through history.
I am a joke and a secret here, and I will leave.
It is morning now. The light whitens her face more than ever.)

THE CHORUS SPEAKS HER WORDS
AS SHE DANCES

You are perishing like the old men. Already your arms are gone,
your legs filled with scented straw tied off at the knees.
Your hair hacked off. How I wish I could take on each part
of you as it leaves. Sweet mouse princess, I would sing
like a nightingale, higher and higher to a screech
which the heart recognizes, which the helpless stars enjoy—
like the sound of the edge of grass.

I adore you. I take you seriously, even if I am alone in this.
If you had arms, you would lift them up I know. Ah, Love,
what knows that?

(How tired and barren I am.)
Mouse eyes. Lady with white on her face. What will the world do
without you? What will the sea do?
How will they remember the almond flowers? And the old man,
smiling, holding up the new lamb: whom will he hold it up to?
What will the rough men do after their rounds of drinks
and each one has told his story? How will they get home
without the sound of the shore any more?

(I think my doll is the sole survivor, my Buddha mouse, moon
princess, amputee who still has the same eyes.
With her song that the deer sings when it is terrified.
That the rabbits sing, grass sings, fish, the sea sings:
a sound like frost, like sleet, high keening, shrill squeak.
Zo-on-na, Kannon, I hold each side of her deeply affected face
and turn on the floor.

THE GIRL I CALL ALMA

The girl I call Alma who is so white
is good, isn't she? Even though she does not speak,
you can tell by her distress that she is
just like the beach and the sea, isn't she?
And she is disappearing, isn't that good?
And the white curtains, and the secret smile
are just her way with the lies, aren't they?
And that we are not alone, ever.
And that everything is backwards
otherwise.
And that inside the no is the yes. Isn't it?
Isn't it? And that she is the god who perishes:
the food we eat, the body we fuck,
the loose net we throw out that gathers her.
Fish! Fish! White sun! Tell me we are one
and that it's the others who scar me,
not you.

A GAME CALLED FEAR

The young cows run in the sound of the river,
making a noise on the grass
clumsy but full of gaiety. Not like the water.
There is the sound of birds in the white air.
The road is wet with rain,
the trees still and quiet.
The young cows are not afraid, I can tell you.
They stop and look together in one direction,
then run to the other end of the field
as if they were playing a game called fear.
The sky is silent and the river is loud
this time of year.

WE MANAGE MOST WHEN
WE MANAGE SMALL

What things are steadfast? Not the birds.
Not the bride and groom who hurry
in their brevity to reach one another.
The stars do not blow away as we do.
The heavenly things ignite and freeze.
But not as my hair falls before you.
Fragile and momentary, we continue.
Fearing madness in all things huge
and their requiring. Managing as thin light
on water. Managing only greetings
and farewells. We love a little, as the mice
huddle, as the goat leans against my hand.
As the lovers quickening, riding time.
Making safety in the moment. This touching
home goes far. This fishing in the air.

PART I

ALMA

FOR JACK GILBERT
IT WAS LIKE BEING ALIVE TWICE

35	Growing Up
36	Summer in a Small Town
37	Unaccountable
38	After That
39	No More Marriages
40	Euridice
42	Now Destroyed
44	The Defeated
46	Too Bright to See
47	The Apparent

PART THREE: AFTER THAT

51	Not Singing
52	Blake
54	The Gods Must Not Know Us
56	The Grub
57	This Place
58	What If the World Stays Always Far Off
61	Staying On
62	Lilith
64	As When the Blowfish Perishing
65	Sun Moon Kelp Flower or Goat
66	Skylord
67	Alma to Her Sister

CONTENTS

PART ONE: ALMA

9 We Manage Most When We Manage Small

10 A Game Called Fear

11 The Girl I Call Alma

12 The Chorus Speaks Her Words As She Dances

14 Gnostics on Trial

15 There She Is

16 The Woman Who Looks for Her Lost Sister
    She Says

17 At the Shore

18 The Beckett Kit

20 Sigismundo

21 The Poet Goes About Her Business

22 Goethe's Death Mask

23 Alma in All Seasons

24 Different Not Less

PART TWO: THE MARRIAGE AND AFTER

27 The Wife

28 The Island of Kos

29 Trouble in the Portable Marriage

30 The Small Lizard

31 Together in Greece

32 Classicism

33 Alma Watching Her Husband

34 Whole and Without Blessing

Copyright © 1981 by Linda Gregg

ACKNOWLEDGEMENTS

Some of the poems in this book were first published in *Antaeus,
Crazy Horse, Iowa Review, The Kenyon Review, The Nation, New Ameri-
can Review, The Paris Review* and *13th Moon*. 'The Beckett Kit,'
'Goethe's Death Mask' and 'A Game Called Fear' originally ap-
peared in *The New Yorker*. 'The Defeated,' 'Sun Moon Kelp Flower
or Goat,' 'Together in Greece,' 'Alma Watching Her Husband,'
'The Wife,' 'The Poet Goes About Her Business,' 'Gnostics on
Trial,' 'This Place,' 'Blake,' 'What If the World Stays Always Far
Off,' 'Too Bright to See,' and 'Lilith' originally appeared in *Iron-
wood*. 'Trouble in the Portable Marriage' originally appeared in
Ploughshares. Some poems are included in THE AMERICAN POETRY
ANTHOLOGY and THE ARDIS ANTHOLOGY OF NEW AMERICAN
POETRY.

Publication of this volume is made possible in part by a grant from
the National Endowment for the Arts.

Library of Congress card number 80-067983
ISBN 0-915308-27-4
      0-915308-28-2 (paper)

FIRST PRINTING, 1981

Published by GRAYWOLF PRESS, Post Office Box 142, Port Town-
send, Washington 98368. All rights reserved.

92194

TOO BRIGHT
TO SEE

POEMS BY LINDA GREGG

GRAYWOLF PRESS

TOO BRIGHT TO SEE